My First Book for
Listening and Speaking

我的第一本
英语听说
入门书 1

丁洁◎著

北京联合出版公司

前言

任何一种有声语言，口语总是第一性的。作为丁洁英语整体教学系列之首的《我的第一本英语听说入门书》是专门为没有学过英语的各个年龄段的中国人写的。对于那些学了多年英语，却不善听说的人们，不妨也可用本书重新唤起自信。

全书是配有英语音频但不见文字的两本连环画册。相信这本历经长期教学第一线的实践写出的教材，将和作者为不同年龄段学生写于不同年代的教材一样，能够获得相同的可喜的教学效果！

归纳起来，本书有以下特点：

1.全书围绕十多个活泼可爱、性格各异的男女学生学英语、品生活的种种趣事而展开。交谈内容都是学习者在日常生活中最急切想获得的基本又实用的对话，更是作者在长期教学实践中根据学生共同遇到的难点、困惑，以及有利日后学习的需要而决定的。录音充分展现英（美）语鲜活地道的语音，和极富节奏动感的语调的美。学生在自然的熏陶和相互感染中学会听声辨音，并拿腔作调地在实践中获得听说能力。

2.语言是和思维密切相连的，其最小单位是句子。全书的连环画犹如连续剧，学生通过直观图像中不同人物用英语交流的表情，配合听有关音频，学会观察思考，从根本上排除汉英两种语言在思维表达形式上的互混和干扰，便捷又简单地学会用英语的思维特点获得听说能力。而且，还能通过图像极大地发挥右脑形象思维、直觉思维、综合理解语言的整体功能，也充分激发着左脑联想、推理、判断、讲话和语言的记忆等功能。显然，这样做有利于开发智力、启迪思维。而这正是培养创造型人才的根本。

3.只有学会思考和善于发现才能获得真正的学习兴趣。它的获得涉及学习的内容和教法的得当。全书的语言功能和话题包括了从礼仪习俗到学习、戏耍等在内的社会交往表达了书中孩子们各自的喜恶爱好、是非判断，也反映出他们心中对师长、父母、兄妹和同学的关爱。尽管内容厚重，累计单词逾四百，但大量的语言输入是通过灵活多样的编排方式进行的，使单词高频率地复现在语言的综合运用中，既避免前背后忘的苦恼，也尽情享受到学习的乐趣。特别是通过书中丁老师对学生的提问，帮助学生学习思考，懂得顺向和逆向思维，或通过归纳总结、分析对比来找出规律。也就是说，用书中学生的具体榜样告知读者应如何积极主动地打开知识的宝库、应如何来掌握科学的学习方法，从而增加自信和学习的乐趣。而兴趣和自信则是最具价值的精神财富。

4.立足培养学生纯正地道、悦耳动听的语音语调。良好的学习习惯举足轻重，为此我们坚决反对全班拉着长调齐声跟读，而是要求每个学生聆听录音或老师教学时，应不出声或出小声地唇动，以便老师逐个观察口型，有的放矢地把那些有错误发音的学生叫到全班面前表演。当错误得到大家指正，受益的是全班学生，勇于实践不怕出错的态度也能得到发扬。我们主张在教学中多用三角提问法把全班结为整体，更有效地发挥每个学生的智力；反对只用"Yes""No"或简单答语来回答老师的提问。我们反对死记硬背课文，但要求在反复多听并熟读每课书的基础上，能融会贯通地脱口而出，学会综合运用语言，提高思维和听说的能力。因此，每天保证用20-30分钟认真听录音，并模仿朗诵，养成听说习惯是完全有必要的。

本书两画册96课需要至少96节课时来完成教学要求。而这恰好是用以培养良好习惯的必要保证。基于全国各地各类学校在起始学习英语的年龄、班级大小，及每学期授课总时数存在的差异，各校可分别用二到四个学期学完本书，使学生获得良好的学习习惯，并具有善听能说的英语能力，为今后的进一步学习奠定扎实的基础。

当你品味画家晓西以其生花妙笔勾画出的幅幅图像，并聆听录音师吕群精心录制的Alex和Anna甜美又富激情的朗诵和吟唱，相信你一定能从中领悟并享受到英语语言的魅力所在。欢迎你的积极参与。行动吧!

❶ 教与学的几个原则

（1）把培养听说和全方位能力结为整体。绝不允许课前预习，而要通过我们设定的每个教学环节，在使学生获得听说能力的同时，提高全方位的能力。

（2）心系全班，切实做到把学和用结为整体。老师应随教学实践对学生的了解为每个学生建档。其内容包括家庭环境、个人的性格特长和爱好，以及学习英语的许多变化进步的细节，以便结合实际，教活所学的语言内容。为此，对于人数过多的班级组，建课后学习小组是必要的，这样做有利于更好地了解学生，有针对性地不断树立变后进为先进的典型，有利于培养干部并争创集体荣誉。

（3）老师配合教学的手势、眼神、表情和动作务必准确明白。这样做有利于学生理解、仿效，使学生们全身心动起来。还可用简单的指向方式，便捷又具体地组织师生间的多角提问。总之，利用课堂四十分钟的分分秒秒，营造全班教学有序、思维敏捷、积极主动、节奏欢快的学习氛围。

（4）牢记英语课上唱英语歌的目的是通过节奏给大脑的刺激，使思维与语言的固有频率引起共振，从而促使记忆。但唱好歌的前提必须是能正确地吐词发音，满足于哼唱小曲般的滥唱只能浪费课时，而无助于获得听说能力。全书依据教学的需要，提供了可供听说、戏耍等不同要求的十多首英语歌曲。如能结合学过的内容，在学会听说的基础上再选唱作者撰写的《101首英语歌曲大家唱》中的有关曲目，定能事半功倍地培养出一批能听说、会演唱，有扎实基本功的英语人才。

❷ 教学的具体步骤和方法

（1）看。在上每一课新书时，先让学生认真仔细地观看有关图像，以便对画面呈现的形象有初步的直觉反映。在刚接触本教材时，可允许学生用母语简述对画面的第一印象，经相互启发来抓住重点。老师绝对不能逐词逐句汉英对译。大约用一两分钟即可。

（2）看听。边看图像、边听录音两三遍。一般占时三四分钟。起始阶段，放听第一遍录音时，应首先配合声音搞清楚图像中出现的男女学生是谁和谁在交谈。他们是如何以彼此的英文名字相称呼的。在放听第二遍录音时，使学习者既形象又直接地通过画面理解声音的意思，以保证声音和图像的协调作用。达到初步整体感知语音、语调、节奏等语句中大约百分之三十的内容。必要时再放听第三遍录音，其目的是配合音和像的紧密结合，了解本课书要学习的内容重点。

（3）看听说演示。演示是课堂教学中最为重要的环节，是决定教学成败的关键。一般每课书都需用25到30分钟来组织教学。按课文逐步演示练习，演示结束后，应再完整地放听全课录音，以加深印象。

在演示过程中，首先应顺应语言的逻辑，针对新课对话中的新单词、习惯用语、主题内容、语言结构等特点，抓住重点、分层次地用由浅入深、以旧带新等方式，逐个进行边推理、边学习、边记忆的讲练演示，可根据需要穿插图像呈现的情景，使学生凭借图像，让语言和意义联系起来。但用图像的目的在于将来摈弃图像，使语言和意义直接联系。因此，必须将画面中要说明的某个词或短语的有关内容和实际中的人和物相互联系，使学生在老师迅速变换的内容方式提问中说出尽可能多、尽可能新、尽可能不重复的话。在交谈的实践中，还应有目的地配合听录音，加深学习者注意语音语调和表情达意的关系，从而更进一步理解，达到基本掌握某个新单词的发音、意义和在语句中相应的功能。使学生听到有关的"音"，就能直接感知其语言的涵义。

（4）听说演唱。用时约五六分钟。演示结束，由老师根据演示过程中对学生的了解，及时组织表演，反馈学习掌握的情况。为让每个学生都能因各自展现的才华受到肯定而享受到学习的乐趣，还应允许有的学生在课后再作准备，自行分配角色，于第二天上课时进行表演。重视平时的表演，将其作为学期重要的考核成绩。期末考试表演的内容方式可由师生共同议定。既为老师近距离了解学生、进行具体指导创造机会，又能增进师生间的互信，有效发挥学生综合运用语言的能力和组织能力。

丁洁于2012年8月

目录

Contens

16

44

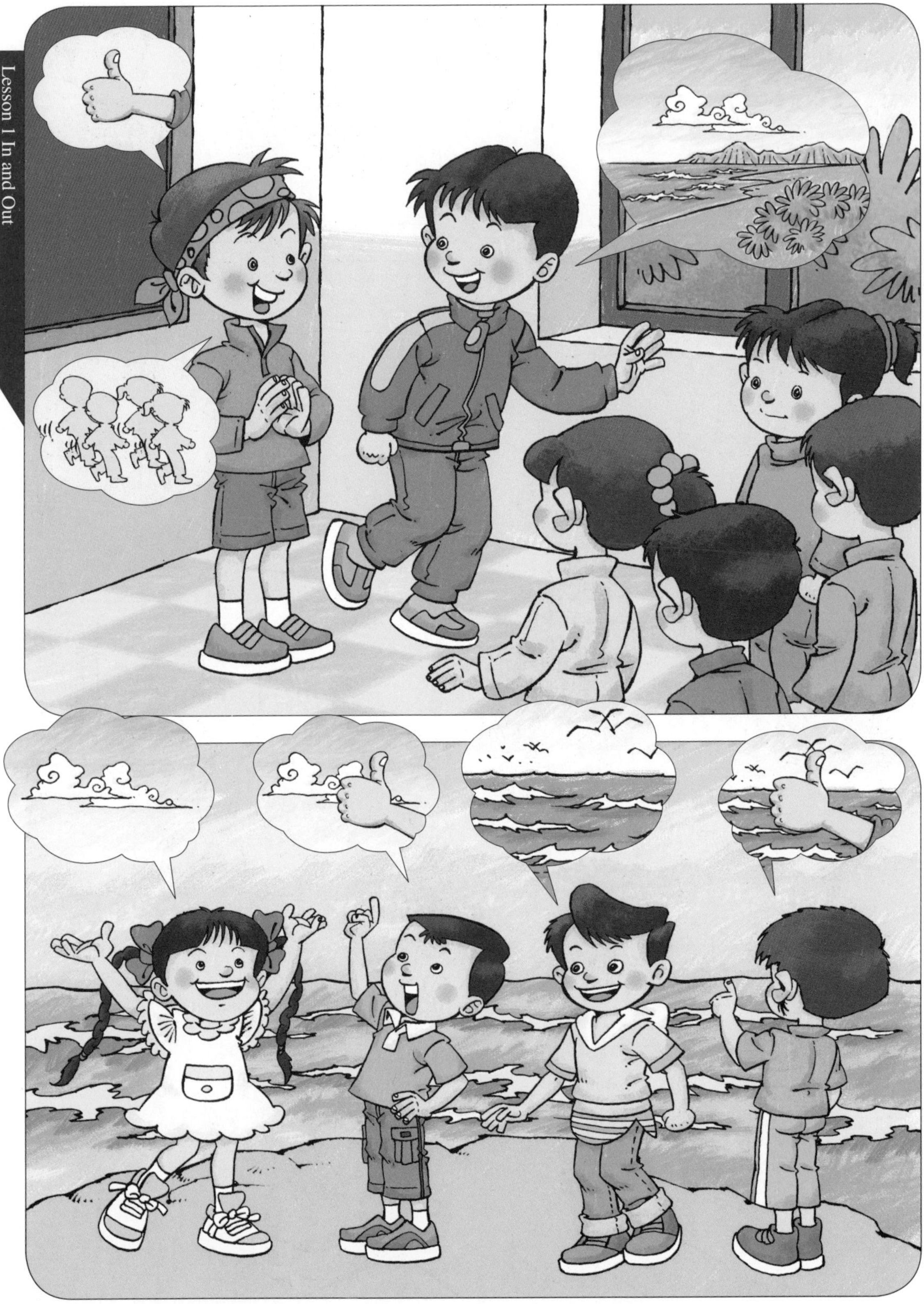

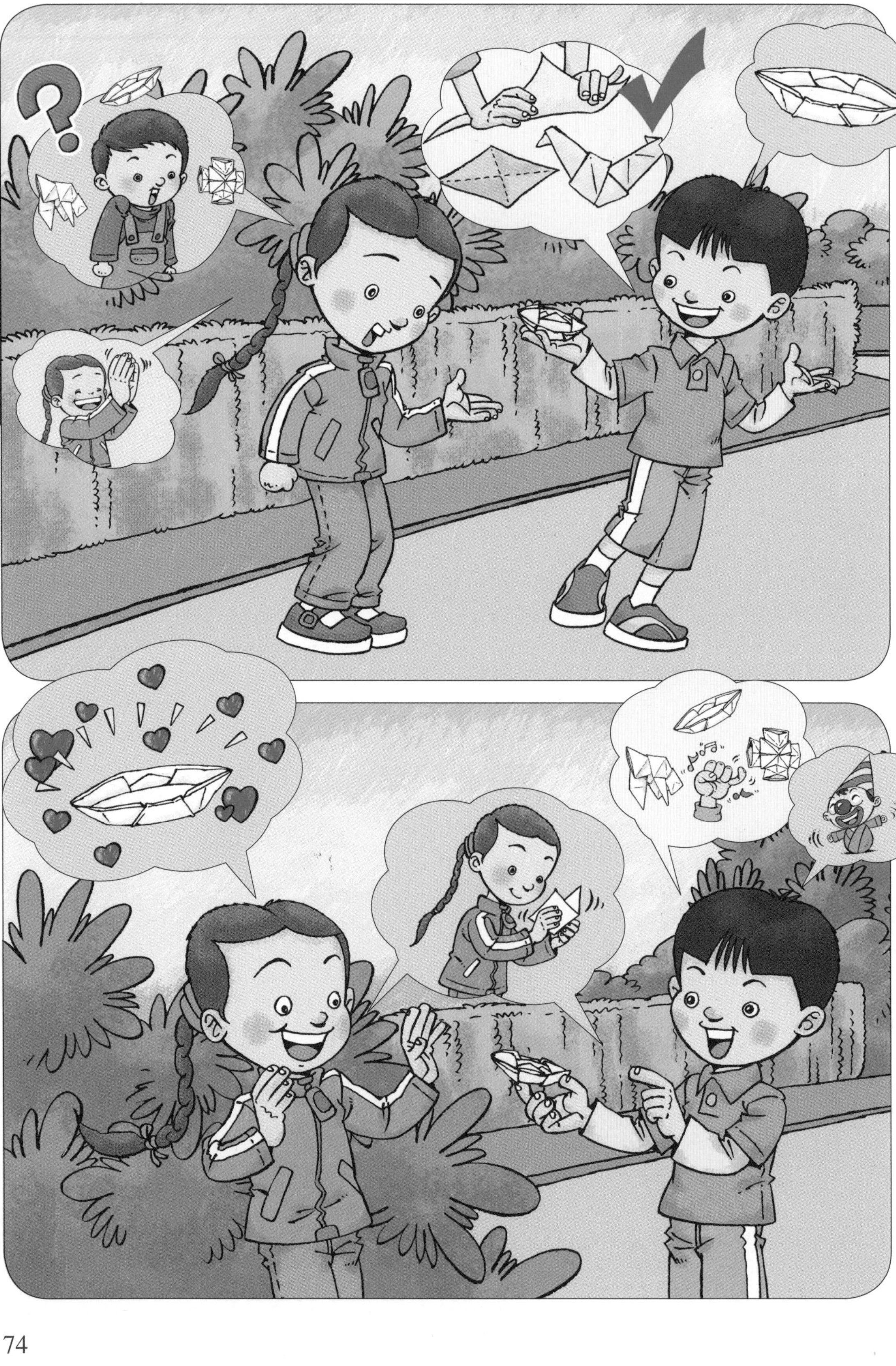

86

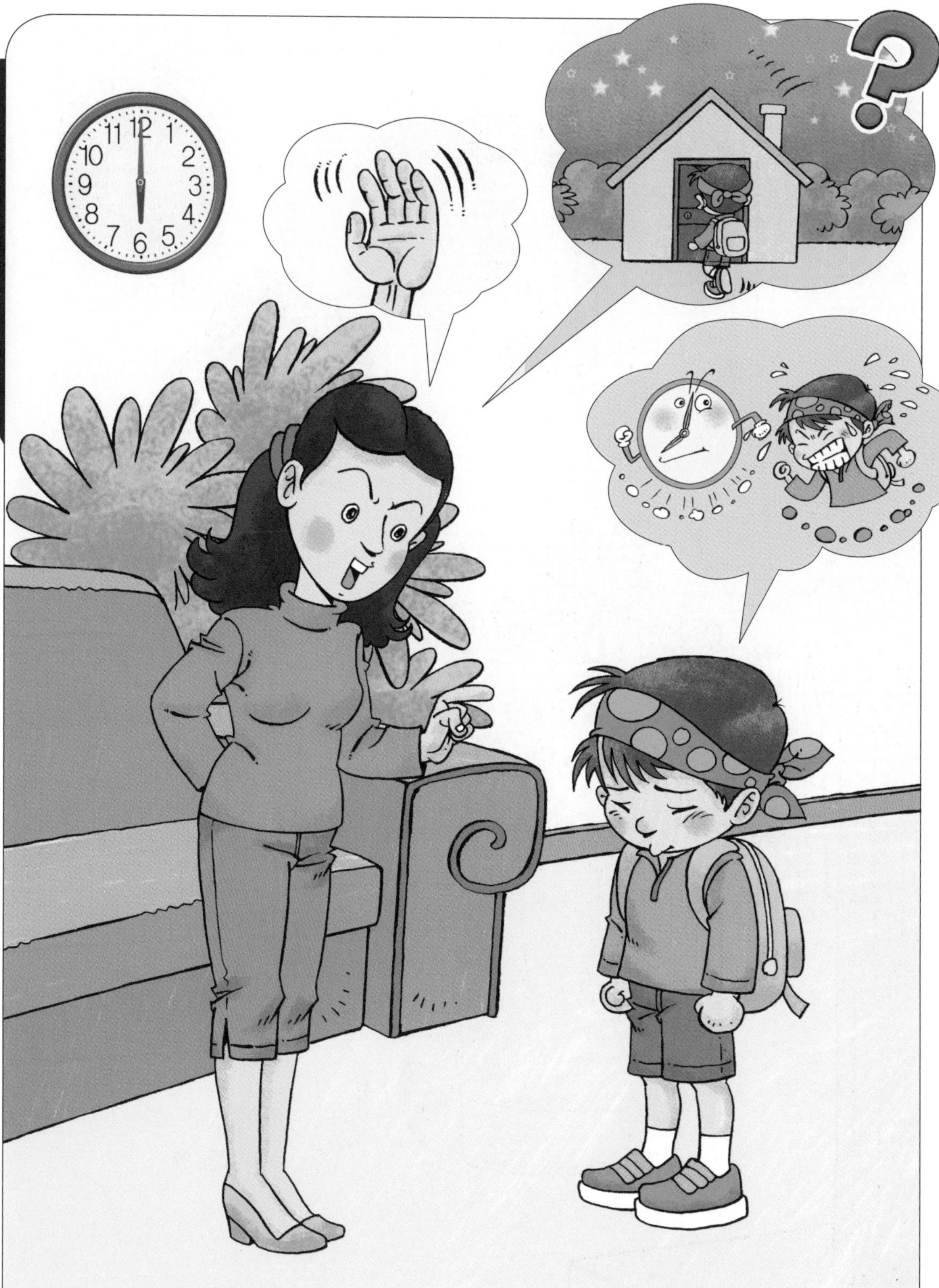

附　录

Unit 1 Greetings
Lesson 1 Welcome

Isaac: Welcome.
All: Welcome, welcome.
Hope: Welcome to our school.
Jane: Welcome.
All: Welcome.
Steve: Welcome to our class.

Lesson 2 How Are You Doing?

Eva: Hi, Tom. How are you doing?
Tom: Great. How are you doing, Eva?
Eva: Super. How are you doing, Steve?
Steve: Great. How are you doing, Amy?
Amy: Super great.

Lesson 3 Good Morning

Hope: Good morning, Ms. Ding.
Ms. Ding: Good morning, Hope.
Hope: Good morning, Mr. Lee.
Mr. Lee: Good morning, Hope.

Ms. Song: Good morning, Mr. Lee.
Mr. Lee: Good morning, Ms. Song. How are you?
Ms. Song: I'm fine, thank you. How are you?
Mr. Lee: I'm fine too. Thank you.

Lesson 4 Good Afternoon

Amy: Good afternoon, Hope. How are you doing?
Hope: I'm doing fine, thank you. How about you?

Amy: I'm very well. Thank you too.

James: Hi, Ulysses. How are you doing this afternoon?
Ulysses: Very well, thank you. How about you?
James: Super. Thank you.

Lesson 5 My Name Is...

Jane: Hi, my name is Jane.
James: Hello, my name is James.
Eva: My name is Eva.
Steve: Hi guys. My name is Steve.
Ida: Hello, my name is Ida.
Isaac: My name is Isaac.
Hope: Hello, my name is Hope.
Tony: My name is Tony.
Judy: Hello, my name is Judy.
Ulysses: Hi, my name is Ulysses.

Lesson 6 Your Name, Please?

Kent: My name is Kent. Your name, please?
Alan: My name is Alan. What's your name?
Kate: My name is Kate. Your name, please?
Helen: My name is Helen.
All: (Singing together)
My name is Kent.
My name is Kate.
My name is Alan.
My name is Helen.
Hi Kent; Hi Kate; Hi Alan; Hi Helen

Lesson 7 What Is Your Name?

Isaac: Welcome to our school.

Hope: Welcome to our class. I'm Hope. What's your name?

Alex: My name is Alex. What's your name again?

Hope: Hope.

Alex: Nice to meet you, Hope.

Hope: Nice to meet you too, Alex.

Isaac: My name is Isaac. What's your name?

Anna: My name is Anna. Glad to meet you.

Isaac: Glad to meet you too.

Lesson 8 Nice to See You

Hope: Hi. Good morning, James.

James: Hello, Hope. How are you doing this morning?

Hope: I'm doing fine, thank you. It's nice to see you again.

James: Nice to see you too.

Adam: Hi! My name is Adam, a new pupil.

James: My name is James. Welcome to our class, Adam. It's nice to meet you.

Adam: Nice to meet you too.

Lesson 9 Let's Be Good Friends

Elizabeth: Hello. I'm Elizabeth. What's your name?

Tony: I'm Tony. It's nice to meet you, Elizabeth.

Elizabeth: Nice to meet you too, Tony.

Tony: Let's be good friends.

Elizabeth: Yes. Let's be good friends.

Lesson 10 Goodbye

Steve: Hello, James, my friend. How are you doing this morning?

James: Hi, I'm doing fine. How are you, Steve?

Steve: Great! Oh, I have to say goodbye to you now. Nice seeing you again.

James: Nice seeing you too. Goodbye. Have a good day.

Steve: Bye-bye. Have a nice day. See you soon.

Amy: Hi, Hope. How are you doing this afternoon?

Hope: I'm very well, thank you. How about you?

Amy: I'm fine too. Thank you. Goodbye. Have a good day.

Hope: Nice seeing you, my friend. Have a good day. Bye-bye.

Lesson 11 What's His/Her Name?

Ms. Ding: Now let's listen to a new song. (The sound of singing)

Ms. Ding: How many pupils' names do you hear? No, you are wrong. Let's listen to the song again. Now, you are right. You all are right.

Ms. Ding: Now let's listen to the second verse of the song. Pay attention to the words.
What's his name? His name is Mike.
What's her name? Her name is Ruth.
What's his name? His name is Mark.
What's her name? Her name is Rose.

Ms. Ding: What's his name?

Hope: His name is Steve.

Ms. Ding: What's her name?

Isaac: Her name is Amy.

Ms. Ding: Now listen to the song once again. What are the names of the two boys? And what are the names of the two girls?

Steve: The two boys' names are Mike and Mark. The two girls' names are Rose and Ruth.

Ms. Ding: Very good.

Lesson 12 Asking Each Other's Names

Ms. Ding: Now let's listen to the dialogue first. Then answer my questions.

A: Hello, little boy. What's your name?

B: My name is Tony. Tony. Hello, little girl. What's your name?

B: My name is Elizabeth.

Ms. Ding: What's the little boy's name in the dialogue?

James: His name is Tony.

Ms. Ding: What's the little girl's name?

Amy: Her name is Elizabeth.

Ms. Ding: What's his name? (Pointing to a boy)

Jane: Your name, please?

Bob: My name is Bob.

Jane: His name is Bob, Ms. Ding. Bob is Tom's good friend.

Ms. Ding: Good job. What's his name? (Pointing to another boy)

Tom: His name is Kate.

All: (Laughing)

Tom: Sorry. Kate is a girl's name. His name is Kent. Kate is his sister.

Ms. Ding: Very good.

Unit 2 Greetings
Lesson 1 Happy Holiday

Hope: Happy holiday to you all.

Ulysses: Happy holiday to you!

Steve: Happy holiday.

Eva: I'm happy. Are you happy?

Jane: I'm very happy.

Ida: I'm happy too.

James: We are all very happy.

Hope: Let's go to see Ms. Ding.

All: Yes. Let's go.

Hope: Happy holiday. This flower is for you, Ms. Ding.

Ms. Ding: Thank you for the pretty flower. Now let's sing this song "Happy Holiday" together. This song is for you all. (Singing)
Happy, happy, happy holiday.
Happy holiday.
Happy, happy, happy holiday.
This song (flower) is for you.

Lesson 2 I Miss You

Tom: Gee, I'm glad we are back in school. Glad to see all my friends again. You look wonderful, Tony.

Tony: You look great too. I miss you and all my friends very much.

Tom: Me too.

Lesson 3 Who Is She/He?

Amy: Who is the little girl? Who is she?

Ida: She is Vicky. She is my friend.

Amy: Who is the little boy? Who is he?

Ida: He is David. He is Vicky's brother.

Amy: Is Vicky a pupil?

Ida: Yes, she is. She is Ms. Ding's pupil.

Amy: Is David in school?

Ida: No, he isn't. He is not in school.

Lesson 4 Who Is Ms. Ding?

Diana: Who is Ms. Ding?

Hope: She is my English teacher. She is my friend too.

Diana: Who is Kent?

Hope: He is my classmate.

Diana: Is Kate your classmate too?

Hope: No, she isn't. She is my friend. She is in Class Two. I'm in Class One.

Diana: I see. She is your schoolmate.

Hope: Kent is her brother. Ms. Ding is our English teacher.

Lesson 5 Good Evening

Vicky: Good evening, mom and dad. Good evening, David. Good evening to you all.

All: Good evening, Vicky.

Lesson 6 Good Night

David: Good night, mom. Good night, dad.

Mom: Good night, boy. Have a good dream.

Dad: Good night, sonny. Have a good dream.

David: Have a good dream, mom and dad.

Lesson 7 At 8 in the Evening

Mr. Zhang: Good evening, Ms. Liu.

Ms. Liu: Good evening, Mr. Zhang. How are you doing this evening?

Mr. Zhang: Not bad.

Ms. Liu: Is my son, Adam, in here?

Mr. Zhang: Oh yes. He is. Adam and Steve, come here, please.

Adam: Good evening, Uncle Zhang. Good evening, Mom.

Steve: Good evening, Auntie Liu. Good evening, Dad.

Ms. Liu: Good evening. Oh, it's eight, late in the evening. Adam, say good night to Uncle Zhang and Steve.

Adam: Good night, Uncle Zhang. Good night, Steve.

Steve: Good night, Auntie Liu. Good night, Adam.

Mr. Zhang: Good night, Ms. Liu. Good night, Adam.

Ms. Liu: Good night, Mr. Zhang. Good night, Steve.

Lesson 8 Sorry, I'm Late

Ms. Ding: Good morning, boys and girls. It's time for class.

All: Good morning, Ms. Ding.

Ms. Ding: Oh, Tom is absent.

Tom: No, I'm here. Sorry, Ms. Ding, I'm late.

Ms. Ding: Yes, you are late.

All: (Singing)

One two three four; Come in, please. Come in, please. And shut the door. Five six seven eight; It's time for school.

And you are very late. You are very late. Nine ten, nine ten; don't be late for school again.

Ms. Ding: Now come on in and shut the door.

Lesson 9 It's Ok

Ms. Ding: Now let's play a game.

All: Great! Let's play.

Tom: Pass me the ball!

Kent: Pass me the ball!

Tom: Oh, sorry, I'm so sorry. Did I hurt you?

Kent: Are you hurt?

Ms. Ding: Are you hurt, Amy?

Amy: No. I'm ok. It's all right. I am fine.

Lesson 10 Please Do Me a Favor

Tom: Will you please do me a favor?

Steve: (No answer)

Tom: Will you please do me a favor? I need your help. Please help me. Help me please!

Steve: Well, how can I help you?

Lesson 11 You Are Pretty

Hope: Good morning, Helen. You are very pretty this morning.

Helen: Thank you. You are pretty too.

Hope: Thank you.

Helen: Hi, Ulysses. How are you doing this morning?

Ulysses: Super, and you?

Helen: Not bad. Thank you. You are very smart, Ulysses.

Ulysses: Thank you. You are too.

Helen: Thank you. It's very nice of you.

Lesson 12 Thanks

Tom: Thank you for helping me.

Steve: You're welcome.

Tom: Thank you so much for your great help.

Steve: You're very welcome.

Tom: Let me say thanks again.

Steve: Oh, don't mention it. We are friends.

Tom: Yes, we are. So thanks again, my friend.

Steve: It's my pleasure.

Tom: Thank you.

Steve: Thank you.

Unit 3 Daily Life
Lesson 1 In and Out

Isaac: Let's get out and play.

Tom: Great! Let's go.

Amy: Wow, the sky is so blue.

Tony: Yeah, the sky is very blue.

Ulysses: And the sea is blue, too.

Eva: Yeah, the sea is blue, too.

Isaac: Now let's learn to sing a new song first. Then play a game.

All: (Singing)
One, two, sky blue. All in, all in but you.
One, two, sky blue. All out, all out but you.
One, two, blue sea. All in, all in but me.
One, two, blue sea. All out, all out but me.

Steve: So we can learn as we play.

Lesson 2 Red and Green Light

Vicky: Please stop, David. Look out! The light is red!

David: Oh, my! Red light! Stop.

Vicky: Look! The light is green now. We can go!

David: Oh, good. Green light! Let's go.

Amy: Come here, Vicky and David. I'm here. Come over here please.

Lesson 3 We Go Rolling the Hoop

David: Let's go rolling the hoop.

Tom: Great. Let's go rolling the hoop.

David: The hoop is round.

Isaac: Together with friends, we go rolling the hoop.

David: We go rolling and rolling and rolling the hoop.

All: We like rolling the hoop together with our friends.

Isaac: We go rolling the round hoop around and around, around and around.

Lesson 4 We Go Jumping the Rope

Jane: I don't like rolling the hoop. I like jumping the rope.

Amy: I like jumping the rope too.

Jane: Then let's go jumping the rope.

Vicky: Ok. Here's a rope turning rhyme. Listen, please.

Miss. Miss, pretty little Miss.
Jump in and out. Jump in and out.
Keep the rope turning;
Keep the rope turning;
When you miss, pretty little Miss,
Out you go, if you miss like this.

Jane: Oh, that's a good rhyme. Let's say the rhyme and jump the rope.

Lesson 5 Have a Ball (1)

Isaac: Have a ball, please. I have a ping-pong ball. I like playing ping-pong.

Ulysses: I have a ping-pong ball, too.

Steve: I have a golfball. My father likes playing golf.

Hope: I have a volleyball. I like playing volleyball. Jane likes playing volleyball too.

Kent: I have a basketball. I like playing basketball. Isaac and Tony like playing basketball too.

Steve: Me too.

Lesson 6 Have a Ball (2)

Diana: I have a baseball. My brother and I like playing baseball.

Tom: I have a football. I like playing football. Who else likes playing football?

Judy: Ida, Vicky and I like playing football.

Tom: You girls like playing football too?

Girls: Why not?

Lesson 7 I Can Read and Write

Ms. Ding: I can read and write. Who can read? Who can write?

Helen: I can read. I can write.

Kent: I can read and write.

(So many pupils are raising hands while saying "Me, too" and "I can".)

Steve: We can read and we can write.

Ms. Ding: Good. But right now you can't read and write English. I can dance. Can you dance?

Hope: You can dance. I can dance, too.

Isaac: I can sing, but I can't dance.

Ms. Ding: Can Amy sing? Can Tom dance?

Ulysses: She can sing, but he can't dance.

Lesson 8 Come, Dance with Me

Ms. Ding: Come, friends. Dance with me, please.

Two rows and face to face.

Give me your two hands.
Heel and toes; heel and toes.
Turn around. Away we go.
We are the merry row.

Hope: Come on, boys and girls. Let's dance together.
Two rows and face to face.
Give me your two hands.
Heel and toes; heel and toes.
Turn around. Away we go.
We are the merry row.

Lesson 9 In a Ballroom

Ms. Ding: Boys and girls, come here, please. This ballroom is very pretty.

Tom: Yeah, a very pretty ballroom. Let's play football here.

Kent: Oh, no. Let's play volleyball.

Tony: No. Let's play basketball.

Ulysses: No way! Let's play ping-pong.

Ms. Ding: No, you can't play ball in a ballroom, but we can dance in the ballroom. Come on, boys and girls. Let's dance.

All: Ok. Let's dance in the ballroom.

Lesson 10 We All Like Our School

Amy: I like my school.

Tony: Me too.

Hope: We all like our school.

Steve: At school, we learn and play.

Isaac: At school, we sing and dance.

Hope: We make good progress everyday.

All: Yeah, we make very good progress everyday.

Lesson 11 Let Me Try

Jane: Can you draw, Tony?

Tony: No, I can't. I can't draw.

Jane: Have a try, please.

Tony: Ok. Let me try to draw something. Is it good?

Jane: No, it's not good. Let me help you. See, try again, please.

Tony: Ok. Let me try again.

Jane: Yeah. I believe you will make good progress.

Tony: Thanks. I believe I will.

Lesson 12 Can You Fold Paper?

Vicky: Hi, James. I need your help. Can you fold any paper toys for my little brother, David?

James: Yes. I can. See, this is a paper ship.

Vicky: How nice! I like the paper ship.

James: I believe you can fold too. Have a try. Paper folding is easy and fun.

Vicky: Let me try. It's not a paper ship. What is it?

James: It's a funny paper monkey! You are smart.

Vicky: Thank you very much.

James: You are very welcome.

Unit 4 Daily Life
Lesson 1 We Make Great Art

Ms. Ding: Can you use scissors and glue?

Steve: Yes, I can. I'm very good at using scissors and glue.

Ms. Ding: Can you fold any paper toys?

James: Oh, yes. Vicky and I can fold paper toys.

Vicky: See, here is my paper ship.

Ms. Ding: Good. This is a very nice paper ship.

Vicky: Thank you.

Ida: I can fold paper toys too. See, this is my paper hat.

James: And here is my funny paper monkey.

Ms. Ding: Wow, you all can make great art. You kids are smart.

All: Thank you, Ms. Ding.

Steve: We make great art.

James: We kids are smart.

Lesson 2 We Like English

Steve: I like English. Do you like English, Kent?

Kent: Yes, I do. I like English very much.

Steve: Does your sister, Kate, like English too?

Kent: Oh yes, she does. She likes English very much. She can speak English well.

Steve: So we all like English. From now on, let's try to speak English more.

Lesson 3 On the Way to School

Steve: Hello, James, my friend. How are you doing this morning?

James: Super. How about you?

Steve: Very well, thank you. Let's go to school together.

James: Sure. Let's go.

Steve: You have a cool backpack. I like it.

James: Thanks. Your backpack is nice too.

Lesson 4 Walking

Isaac: Now let's go for a walk.

All: Sure. It's a good idea.

Isaac: I am walking. You are walking.

Ulysses: He is walking. She is walking.

Tony: We are walking.

Isaac: Now, let's run.

All: Ok, let's run. Now we are running.

Kent: I'm running. You're running.

Ida: He is running. She is running.

Eva: We are running.

Isaac: Now stop and jump.

All: Stop and jump.

Isaac: Now let's slide.

Jane: All right. Let's slide, slide.

Isaac: Listen, guys. Let's sing together.
Walking, walking. Walking, walking.
Jump, jump, jump, jump, jump, jump.
Running, running, running, running, running, running.
Now let's slide. Now let's slide.

Lesson 5 Afternoon Tea

Steve: Knock, knock.

James: Who is it?

Steve: It's us: Steve, Vicky, and David, your friends.

James: Come in. Good afternoon, Steve, Vicky, and David. Have some tea?

Steve: Yes, a cup of green tea for me, please.

Vicky: Green tea for me too, please.

James: Ok, green tea for you and Vicky. What about you, David? Have a cup of tea too?

David: No thanks. No tea for me. Can I have some cakes?

James: Sure, some cakes for you.

David: Yes, please. I like cakes.

Lesson 6 Excuse Me

Ms. Ding: Now let's learn a little rhyme "Early to bed".

Go to bed late, stay very small.
Go to bed early, grow very tall.

All: Ok, let's try.

Go to bed late, stay very small.
Go to bed early, grow very tall.

Ms. Ding: Good job. Who…?

Tom: Excuse me.

Ms. Ding: Yes?

Tom: May I go to the washing-room?

Ms. Ding: Yes, you may go.

Lesson 7 What's This?

Tony: What's this? It's a pen. Excuse me.

Charles: Yes?

Tony: Is this your pen?

Charles: No, it isn't.

Tony: Excuse me.

Lily: Yes?

Tony: Is this your pen?

Lily: No, it isn't. Oh, it's my teacher, Ms. Song's pen.

(In the Teachers' office)

Tony: Excuse me, Ms. Song.

Ms. Song: Yes?

Tony: Is this your pen?

Ms. Song: Oh, yes. It is my pen. Thank you very much.

Tony: You are very welcome.

Lesson 8 Don't Watch TV Too Much

Ms. Ma: Stop watching TV now. It's late in the evening.

Tom: No. It's early.

Ms. Ma: Don't watch TV too much. It's time for bed. Remember the rhyme?

Go to bed late, stay very small.
Go to bed early, grow very tall.

Tom: But it's not late and I am tall.

Ms. Ma: You are a naughty boy.

Lesson 9 It's No Excuse

Ms. Ma: Come over here, Tom. You are home late today. Why?

Tom: I was in school late.

Ms. Ma: What? You are late for school again?! It's no excuse. Now your play-time is out.

Tom: You mean I can't go and play?! Oh, Mom, I am very, very sorry.

Lesson 10 I Promise

Tom: I watch TV too much at night, and I can't get up early for school. I know it's not good. I won't do that any more. I'll go to bed early every night, and I'll never be late for school again.

Ms. Ma: Promise?

Tom: Yes, I promise and I mean it.

Lesson 11 I'm Special

Ms. Ding: Good morning, everybody. I am special. You are special. Who else is special?

Hope: I'm special. Tony is special. Amy is special…

Ms. Ding: So everybody is special in his or her own way.

All: Yes, we are all special.

Ms. Ding: Who is smart and bright?

Ulysses: I'm smart and bright.

Ms. Ding: Is Jane smart and bright?

Helen: Yes, she is. Jane is very smart and bright. And I am smart and bright too.

Ms. Ding: Yes, you are cute and smart. Is Amy cute and bright?

Hope: Yes, she is. She is cute and bright.

Ms. Ding: Who is brave and bright?

All: Tom is brave and bright.

Vicky: I am brave too.

Ms. Ding: Now let's listen to a rhyme, "I Am Special".

I am smart and bright.
I can read and write.
I am special. I am special.
She is cute and bright.
She can read and write.
She is special.
Everybody is special.
He is brave and bright.
He can read and write.
He is special. Everybody is special.

Lesson 12 I'm a Little Happy Girl/Boy

Ms. Ding: This is Ann, a new pupil in our class. Let's welcome Ann.

Hope: Welcome you to our class. Now we are classmates. We're very happy.

Ann: I am happy too. I like singing. So let me sing a song for you.
My first name's Ann.
I'm a little happy girl.
I can draw and write.
I like singing and skating.

Ms. Ding: A good song. And you sing very well.

Ann: Thank you very much, Ms. Ding.

Tom: As you know, I can't sing very well. Let me try. Listen, please.
My first name is Tom.
I'm a little happy boy.
I can read and paint.
I like playing football.

James: Well done. You sing well, Tom. Let me learn from you.

Tom: Let's learn from each other. Have a try, please.

James: Ok. Let me try.
My first name is James.
I'm a little happy boy.
I can speak English.
I like folding paper toys.

All: Wonderful.

Ms. Ding: You are all very special.